Bloom
for Yourself

REVISED AND EXPANDED

Books by April Green:

Bloom for Yourself II, Let go and grow
Becoming a Wildflower
Bloom for Yourself Journal

For prints, inspiration, and updates visit:
www.bloomforyourself.co.uk

Bloom
for Yourself

April Green

'There's one of April's poems before every chapter of my book Gracefully You

[...] I'm obsessed with her work'

Jenna Dewan

Cover Artwork:
Xavier Esclusa Trias
www.twopots-design.com
xevi@twopots-design.com

Illustrations:
Bea & Wild
Instagram: @bea.andwild

ISBN–13:978-1527216754
ISBN–10:1527216756

www.bloomforyourself.co.uk

healing is:
allowing flowers to grow
in all the places sadness has touched
inside you.

love, april green

healing the roots

i have bloomed and
flowered
a thousand times in
this lifetime;

(even when my roots
were damaged)

because i let the dying petals fall.

April Green

the unfolding

i had to break—i had to understand all the things inside me that were causing me so much pain.

breathing flowers

the year of healing—of breathing flowers and honouring the truth. writing the past out of my bones like the blue weight of twilight.

the kind year, (the year i was kind to myself).

the year daylight taught me how to walk through every inch of my world as though nothing was holding on and everything was letting go.

April Green

i am beautifully broken
open.

(and this is how the sky must feel
after a storm.)

you only become lost
when you are trying to get somewhere
you were never destined to be.

surrender—let life move through you.

it's easier that way.

April Green

art

when things i used to cling to no longer feed my soul,
i turn them into art. and all the empty, aching spaces
they carved out of me become full again.

April Green

'but how do you settle
into your skin and
learn to love all the places
you tried to send back
to the ocean?' she asked.

'you dive into those places and
trust that they will lead you back
home.'

April Green

i create.

that's how i survive.

moment. by. moment.

lay down.
weep.
heal yourself.

(before you can heal anyone else.)

April Green

sometimes,
we don't always realise
that self-destruction is
tearing away
at the thread of our hearts
until we
sometimes quietly,
sometimes violently
fall apart.

but then: the light breaks through.

and we see again.

April Green

intention

i have come to experience the breath-taking truth
that the universe hears my every thought, *even before
i think it*; and then returns it to me in a sometimes
beautiful, sometimes terrifying way.

April Green

that piece of yourself
that you don't understand:

the raw, vulnerable core
that you sweep under your bones
in the hope it will dissolve with your dreams
by the morning.

that piece needs to be unravelled,
and studied and embraced.

for that piece is the science of you.
it's the alchemy of you—the spark that
defines who you are:

beautifully whole
and breathtakingly enough.

April Green

the invitation

learn how to connect with the truth echoing at the back of your heart. trust that beautiful, melancholic whisper; give it the space to breathe.

for when you are honest about how you are feeling, what you are afraid of, where the pain is: you are at your strongest. and when you speak that truth to another person, you multiply that strength.

this is how you make the deepest connections.

April Green

healing the roots

it is not the pain we carry that hurts us the most: it is the reason for that pain.

so in order to heal, you must be willing to delve deep into your roots and unravel the true cause of your pain.

for it is the act of healing the roots that leads to the most incredible, unconscious act of healing the heart, mind, body, and soul.

April Green

we are never truly alone

this morning, i showered the night from my skin and i asked myself: 'why do we get so lonely? we have dirt on our feet, the wilderness in our hair and salt moving through our bones. then there's the air we breathe—an inhale of anything and everything we want it to be: a prayer, the ocean, an answer.'

so i looked up towards the light of the selfless sun, and i made a promise to myself that i would never forget all the different ways we can be touched when we're alone.

April Green

honour me
with honesty
and
i will give you
my loving hands.

(no matter what your story holds.)

April Green

comparison is not constructive:

you cannot make space for loving yourself
if you are always looking at ways in which
you don't think you measure up.

April Green

there may come a time in your life
when you have nowhere else to fall
but into the hands of something far
greater than yourself.

and

i need you to know that falling
into this place (of surrender)
is one of the most magical falls.

because you un-break.

April Green

it is not only
time
that heals the soul:

it is presence
and patience
and faith
and creativity
and silence
and solitude
and breathing (just breathe).

it is reconnecting with the things
that feed your soul.
the things that bring you back
to your soul.

for it was you who wandered;

but you are coming home now.

April Green

the silence after a storm

one of the greatest lessons i ever heard came from the silence after a storm. as though the roots of the earth were tugging at my soul, begging me to stand still and listen:

'find your path in life.
stay in your power.
move with the earth;

and you will never be crushed by anything outside of your control again.'

April Green

when you let something go

there is always that beautiful moment
of self-realisation:

it is *you* who becomes free.

April Green

a love lesson

i have experienced love in its fullest, most abundant form during the times when i have loved without expecting anything in return.

the believer

when you find a person who trusts and believes in you, keep hold of that person—never let them go. they could be on the other side of the world, or the inside of your heart. the distance means nothing when their energy spills over the ocean like the speed of light and raises you up to kiss the sun.

it's like the spreading of warmth, the breaking of bread.

forget me not

to the introverts—alone in a crowd; tongue-tied and terrified. the ones who have taught themselves how to swallow their voice for fear of it sounding out of place in the open air. i want you to know that i understand every word you want to say. but please— unfold the essence of who you are and wear it on the outside as a fragrance no-one has ever owned before. say 'no' often. without apology. and without explanation. and when they ask you who you are, breathe out your name as though you're breathing life into the parts of them that don't see you for the magnificent, rare flower that you are.

April Green

the storms in your life

sometimes, there is no reason whatsoever other than
the simple truth that the universe just wants to watch
you bloom.

April Green

honesty

i am teaching myself how to look at a person with silent words falling from my eyes like wild orchids:

'i trust you enough to show you who i truly am.'

for i have come to understand that if i don't show a person who i truly am, i am rejecting myself. i am telling them that my true self is not good enough for them to see. and instead, i show them a false self because i think it won't hurt as much if they break the false self.

but it will hurt. it will shatter the soul.

April Green

return to yourself

sometimes it takes losing yourself many times before
you understand that you need yourself more than
you need anyone else.

one

days when you feel so confused you end up looking for something you can't find—like a forgotten language under your tongue, a mark of love upon your skin, a memory. these are the days when the earth is trying to speak to you the most; trying to tell you:

'you are not separate from me: the one who moves the tide, breaks open the sky, and changes the fields to gold. you have simply turned your back on me.'

April Green

the place where it hurts:
that's where the answer sits:

silent. aching. and beautiful.

April Green

the practice

release the negative narrative you hold about yourself (for it is not true); and start directing the compassion and forgiveness you give to others towards yourself.

the reward for this daily practice is that you will learn how to love yourself so much that you will need no validation from anyone else.

the soul's language

fear is a fierce and terrible thing that lives in your head and forces you to think about all the things you can't change, whilst running towards the things you think will change you.

but if you could see fear (the way you can feel fear), you would notice how small it becomes the second you use your power to stay in the present moment.

for it is only in the present moment that the soul's language becomes louder than fear.

April Green

wanting

wanting causes emptiness—it makes you feel as though you lack something; as though you have a hole inside you that needs to be filled. so you try to fill it, but you use something outside of yourself; something that doesn't belong to you, something that only causes more wanting and more emptiness. then you get caught in a never-ending, empty cycle of wanting and aching and searching and breaking until you finally come to learn that the thing you want is an illusion, and the thing you lack is *belief.*

the *belief* that you already have everything you need inside you. that you are already whole, already worthy, and already more than enough—just as you are.

gratitude

i have allowed too many moments to pass without
thanking the earth for carrying me through them.

April Green

i am drawn to the quiet souls

for there is a passion in their hearts
that burns harder than any voice
every could.

April Green

time

this i know—we are more passionately alive when we are living in the present moment.   but so often, we rush away time, wanting something to happen, waiting for something to happen. and do you know that in the waiting you are resisting the present moment, choosing not to live, denying life?

time is but a moment, a heartbeat, a breath. you can't rush any of these things—you can't rush time:

you can only walk alongside it and let it show you how to live with grace.

April Green

flowering

i speak of healing as 'doing the work' because healing is a daily practice—it doesn't happen overnight. it happens by knowing yourself: by being aware of the parts of yourself that are holding you back.

introspection is the backbone of healing, which is to say: go deep within and get truthful with yourself about those parts. for there is a crack of light inside you, like a tender ache; a delicate whisper, just waiting for you to listen and honour the message it is giving you.

healing is about reconciling with yourself every day so that you are happy living with yourself every day.

being with myself, healing myself,
is like a tender gathering, a confession:

to the voice i silenced
when i struggled to be understood

to the body i punished
for the self-perceived flaws

to the heart i took for granted
the scars i tucked away
the pain i kept alive.

being with myself, healing myself
is like an act of forgiveness.

April Green

attachment

i can tell you that your soul will shatter into a million
pieces, (which may take years to put back together)
if you keep holding onto cold hearts in the hope that
they will eventually become warm in your hands.

the practice (ii)

but how do you nurture self-love? how do you hold your worth so high in the air that it becomes untouchable?

accept this as the truth:

you are enough just as you are. you are whole and unique and beautiful, just as you are.

accept it as the truth—say it over and over again until this concept of yourself is pressed into your bones like sacred scripture. and then, in the space of a second, a hundred heartbeats, a year, you will no longer hear or accept anything that does not fit with this vision; this glorious image and likeness that you are.

for you have accepted it as the truth.

April Green

falling in love

for me, falling in love is about surrounding myself
with people who help me fall in love with myself.

.

April Green

one day,
the sky will fall
onto your skin
and you will become
all the prayers
you breathed
into the air.
all the poems
you pressed
into your bones.

and you will say:

'it was written.'

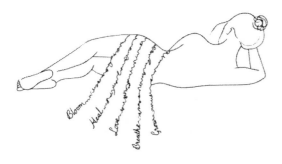

April Green

everything breathes.
everything listens.
even when you don't speak.

the earth is a beating heart.

April Green

to make still the world
and find the spirit of yourself
in the silence.

to me: that is the art of being.

that is the poem.

April Green

inward

the belief that you have to prove your worth to others is a belief that you have carried around with you for too long.

the time has come for you to sit with yourself, nurture yourself, and celebrate yourself.

(never forget that you are here to create the most loving habitat—within yourself.)

April Green

the light within you
doesn't depend on other people:

i have watched you come alive
during moments of great stillness

and i can only imagine that these are
the moments when your soul is
remembering:

'i am a woman honouring my truth,
sharing the flowers of my soul, and
learning that every step i take
is paving a path for all the women
walking behind me.'

—note to self | after the storm

April Green

it is strong roots
that will help you weather
the pull of the world —
(the hunger and the aching
for something more
than you think you are).

and it is strong roots
that will ground you into
realising you are already
so much more than enough,
just as you are.

April Green

and some days
still feel painful.
like the weight of winter
climbing into the heart
of summer.

these are the
resting days.

the days when i
call upon the tiniest
fragment of light
to remind me that
i survived after all.

April Green

detachment

some of us feel everything so deeply that it can be difficult to find balance in everyday life. but what we must remember is that all feelings are transient: they are not supposed to last forever.

so try to honour the feelings that arise within you without feeding those feelings with fear or attaching any meaning to them.

acknowledge them, give them the space to breathe, become free.

then allow the next moment to arrive.

April Green

my desire to be alone
is not a lonely choice, or a selfish
choice.

my desire to be alone is my own.

April Green

the silence of light

i don't think i am as much gifted as i am brave: to break open ribs and write what is hiding inside. to breathe a heavier kind of air and draw it to the silence of light.

April Green

and
just when i think
i know myself
another voice
speaks.
like the echo
of a woman
i have yet to meet.

(and i am learning to answer her call.)

April Green

heartbreak

the most startling thing about heartbreak is in the looking back and noticing that the world didn't actually end.

tender reminders

there are flowers in me
i've forgotten to water:
dreams i once had
plans i once mapped out.

still living.
and breathing.

like tender reminders.

April Green

the greatest teacher
is yourself.
and
the greatest journey
is the one you take
returning fully
to yourself.

April Green

remember:
it is your heart.
only you can nurture it.
only you can help it
bloom.

April Green

at the root of your problems
are people who feel exactly the same.

—find them.

your strength is determined,
not by the things you choose to carry,
but by the things you choose to set
free.

April Green

saltwater

always remember this—you did not come here to ask for forgiveness. you came here as a gift of the purest, rawest form; carrying nothing but the taste of salt on your lips and alchemy in your bones. and if the ash you leave behind is as small as a grain of sand then it will still leave a crushingly beautiful stain of gold upon the earth. so please—practice speaking without an apology falling from your mouth like an afterthought.

because you are just as precious as everyone else.

April Green

you are allowed
to walk away
from anything that
doesn't feel right.

and
perhaps
the thing you
need
the most
is the thing you must
give
the most.

(love/compassion/gratitude/forgiveness.)

April Green

stop burying the parts of yourself
that you don't understand.

the earth will just keep returning them
until you plant them into something that will
grow.

April Green

if there is pain in
your life — you have to be brave.
you have to meet it.

April Green

you become
more and more
beautiful
when you stop trying
to become
someone else.

April Green

sadness

try not to allow the sad person within you to sit with you for too long. for they will become your eyes in the present moment; and the beauty of the miracle before you will be tainted.

don't water down your
uniqueness
for anyone.
be like a wildflower —
passionate and
unforgettable.

(grow in places they never expected.)

April Green

it matters to you.
(that is the most important
thing to remember.)

one night,
the moon will shine
a little bit brighter and
you will forget
you are alone.

April Green

sometimes
it doesn't happen
the way you expect
it to.

(sometimes that's a blessing.)

April Green

keep close
the ones who believe
in you.

April Green

when you learn
how to love yourself
you will never be called
'difficult to love'
again.

April Green

do not chase the breeze.
let the breeze come to you;
whispering all the answers,
carrying you in the right direction.

because, chasing something
creates a storm:

things get broken.

April Green

speaking too softly
or not at all
or loud like a raging storm
is something you are entitled to do.
because the space you have been given
is yours.

and if another person doesn't accept
all of you
then it is because they haven't yet
used their bare, bleeding hands
to dig deep and accept all of
themselves.

so keep being you.

because your authenticity
is teaching others how to be
themselves.

April Green

happiness

(i)

do not put your happiness into someone else's hands. for you will spend your days, *months, years* searching for it in everything you touch.

(ii)

when you make a conscious choice to be happy—no-one can take it away from you because no-one gave it to you.

you gave it to yourself.

April Green

fragile things that break in the wrong hands:

self-worth.

promises.

hearts.

flowers.

letting go is:

letting the emotion of a past experience go.

then you are free to put your energy
into the present moment.

free to create your future
without any attachment
to the shadow of the past.

April Green

wildflower —

keep unfolding
in front of people's eyes.

(without apology.)

April Green

love what you love.

hold onto it
with every atom
of your being.

because what you love
is the reason you exist.

April Green

solitude is not selfish.

it is essential.
it is self-love.

April Green

pay attention
to the things that make you
feel more alive.

(whatever your soul is drawn to will tell you exactly
who you are.)

April Green

to the ones
who feel too much —

make art.

and if they leave —
just grow flowers
in all the empty spaces.

for they were simply
preparing your earth
for sweeter things.

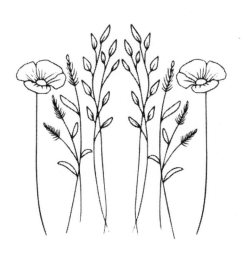

April Green

without dreams:

you will die.

like a flower without rain.
like a day without light.

April Green

you deserve more
of the things that fear
is keeping you from
seeing.

do not fill
the emptiness in your heart
with people
and call it love.

when you cleanse
and clear
old patterns and beliefs,
make sure you fill that space
with fresh flowers, new beginnings,

so that the old life has no place to return.

April Green

when the ache comes:

feed it with flowers
and poems.

a love note:

please find the courage
to live the life *you* want.

because it is your life.

(and you must never forget this.)

April Green

it is only when you surrender
that healing enters your bones
and
starts to do its beautiful work.

April Green

spend time
with the real ones.
the raw ones with
dreams
dripping from their bones
like wild honey.

(the ones still living while they're alive.)

April Green

finding love

do not close yourself off
from love.
do not hide away
from love.

love everything.

the little things.
the inhales.
the moments of life.

listen to
the space between the words
you don't hear.

listen to
the silence.

the beating heart.

the eyes of the
soul.

April Green

some memories
never leave your bones.
like salt in the sea,
they become part of you.

and you carry them.

April Green

if you love a thing
that stops you from
loving yourself:

you have to let that thing go.

April Green

the judgements
you make about yourself
have no substance.

(stop believing them.)

April Green

the life beneath
the life you are wearing
is the one you must listen to
the most.

April Green

that wildness inside you
where the salt in your bones
moves like the tide
and
you loosen your grip
on the earth —

don't run from what wildness.

April Green

the most beautiful
thing a woman can do is
simply love herself.

breathe softer.
and quieter.
and with more intention
to live harder.

.

April Green

a person will show
you how to love them by the
way they love themselves.

April Green

you cannot heal
the thing
you keep hiding
beneath
your bones.

April Green

you can *and will*
be loved
just as you are.

be beautifully free and fearless

stop letting yourself down before you are let down just because you think it is easier to hurt yourself than it is to be hurt.

in protecting yourself, you are closing yourself off from living the life you deserve.

the art of living

you can have balance and serenity in your life.
you can have whatever you ask for.

but good things are only given to you when you
make space for them.

April Green

i hope that the day you find the strength to breathe
and start again, is the day that you understand you
can make your own rules:

you are allowed to sit in solitude without
explaining yourself.

you are allowed to weep until the moon falls down
and the sun rises.

you are allowed to heal at your own pace,
and forgive when you choose.

you are allowed to leave some people and things
behind.

you are allowed to make as many positive beliefs,
and as many healthy boundaries as you choose.

April Green

it is not your
responsibility
to prove
you are enough
for somebody
else.

(just being yourself is enough.)

April Green

always remember
just how rare you are — there is
no-one quite like you.

April Green

reaching the sun

some mornings
when the earth is still asleep
and the breeze drifts across my skin
like a whisper from god,
i crawl inside the stillness of dawn
and inhale her fragrant flowers.

then i pray that a
wilderness of soft mercy
will hold me as i rise.

April Green

the calling

when life opens its doors to you—when a breeze sweeps through your bones like a thousand falling feathers—you must find the courage to take what's yours and fly.

because, life shouldn't be just about surviving.

life should be about feeling every breath passing through your lungs as though it's a symphony only for you.

April Green

growth

it happens when you make a deep connection with
something like art, music, poetry, another soul. it
swells inside you like a deep breath, as though
another person is living beneath your ribs; waking
from a long sleep. then the air you breathe starts to
carry more value, and nothing else matters because
this deep connection is bringing you back to life—
pulling you into a world that seems familiar and
strange and terrifying all at once.

growth is like the splitting of atoms—it expands you
to the point of no return.

April Green

no matter the pain
it has taken you to get here;
the love you have lost,
given up on, passed by.
the wars you have fought,
run from, chased after.

you are still the expanse of sky.
you are still the air,
the earth,
the moving tide,
and everything in between.

it is your birthright
to grow and ache
and change and learn
and hurt and heal.

love.

breathe.

you belong here.

April Green

when inner wisdom speaks
to you —
lean into that space and listen.

because growth lives there:

in the early morning light
in the fractured space between
the calling of your deeper self and
your ability to close yourself off
from the outside world and
connect with that call.

April Green

seeds of dreams

'but how do i grow with all this sadness planted inside my bones?' she asked.

'you grow the way some of the strongest flowers grow,' i said. 'when the darkness is most upon them; amongst the silence of stars—each one like a prayer pressed into the sky.

and then in no time, they awaken in the very earth they used to dream about breaking through.'

April Green

whatever parts of me
you are drawn to
are simply reflections of those parts
already within you.

all i am giving you is the gift of awareness.

April Green

i am starting to fold
the voice of the past
into the palm of my hand

quietly.
like a whisper.
and
without hesitation.

for i am no longer the years behind me:

i am the woman i decide to be
in the very next breath.

April Green

some flowers only bloom once.

and sometimes that's enough
to create a single, breath-taking
moment
that can change a person's life
forever.

April Green

we are loved

the most striking thing i ever saw her wearing was the future in her eyes. even when the ache in her heart walked into a room before she did. even when the sadness swelled inside her like a wave about to spill from the seam of her skin. it was the life still alive in her eyes that drew me towards her. and when she spoke to me, the salt in her voice was not of her own, but of a million women before her whispering the same thing:

'it is because we are loved that we carry the weight of the world and still keep going.'

stay grounded

it doesn't have to be all or nothing:

once you reconnect with yourself—with the earth beneath your feet, the wild against your skin—the middle ground becomes magical and ever expanding.

(sometimes there is more action in stillness than there is in running from yourself in search of stillness.)

the intention to change

change starts with the smallest of steps. but before you even take that first step, you must have the desire, the feeling, the intention to change.

for it is the intention to change that delivers the inspiration.

the universe does the rest.

April Green

wild woman:

do not be afraid to dance alone.

(the earth has been waiting for you.)

April Green

listening to silence

i am certain that if you can walk beneath the breath of life, and keep walking with it, wherever it takes you—then you will have a beautiful life.

we let go by giving ourselves
the space to forgive ourselves.

we let go by giving ourselves
the space to breathe. new. air.

April Green

the earth needs to feel you

the most tragic thing a woman can do is
feel undeserving of the space they take up;
make themselves smaller, shrink.

you must learn to rise every morning
with the unapologetic belief that the
air you breathe belongs to you as much as it
belongs to anyone else.

April Green

and each time i feel myself
breaking a little more;
i tell myself:

'you are not breaking.

you are expanding,

softening. opening.'

(growth nearly always happens on the inside first.)

April Green

the taste of rain

do you remember the time someone made you feel as though you were not good enough: that your dreams were as high as the sky, as far as the moon, and as vast as the stars; and you believed them? so you built a wall around yourself. and you don't remember whether it was to block out their voices, or hold back the moon, or hide from those dreams; but you stayed there. like a dying season. like a sheltered heart.

well i promise that one day you are going to wake up and taste a different kind of sweetness in the rain. one day you are going to rise with the honey gold balm of the sun and ask yourself:

'what if it is more painful to stay here than it is to climb that wall like a fearless rose?'

April Green

brave one:

show them how
you keep rising
and growing.

even when it hurts.

April Green

the scent of living in the moment

and are the greatest moments the ones we aren't expecting, the ones we don't have time to name? for they come, and they touch us like the breeze of butterfly wings; and then they leave us. like little earthquakes. like fading dreams.

and we can't quite put these moments into words, but the soul moves. we transform.

April Green

and i have learned that
every flower gets what
it reaches out for.

April Green

heart waves

we are always being guided towards the things that
are good for us; away from the things that are not.

trust the energy sweeping over your heart.

trust yourself to move in the right direction.

and the moon
looked down at her
and said:

'you are too full
of everything
that makes you whole
to ever be loved
in halves.'

April Green

the buried life

your evolution beings the second you release from your body all the pieces you have denied. all the fragments of truth you have hidden in your darkest corners.

the buried life holds the secret to your greatest transformation.

there is nothing more sacred,
more empowering, more beautiful,
than very slowly becoming
the woman i was intended to be.

April Green

women who love
themselves
are some kind of magic

for they will walk through
every changing season
and learn something new
about themselves each time.

April Green

pressed flowers

i think if you can learn to forgive yourself for the way you dealt with the lessons of the past—get to know the parts of yourself you tucked away in shame, like scars you tried to fold back into the bones of you; then i think that's when your life starts to change.

i think that's when you begin to feel everything so very tenderly.

and the scars become footprints in a path you once honoured, flowers you once pressed.

April Green

the spirit guides

messengers choose you; find you when your voice is lost amongst the weight of the day and your lungs are stretched tight around a life you find yourself wearing. and then a poem, a song, another human soul can give you the answer as though it has travelled a great distance to fall at your feet.

(if you believe in messengers they will always find a way to reach you.)

April Green

and if you're not ready
to bloom for them,
(to show them who you really are)
then bloom for yourself.
bloom internally.
bloom so much that buds fall from your bones
and earth breaks beneath your feet.

April Green

change is like a sacred season,
a natural expansion, stepping
forwards.

but sometimes the hard season
will return again and again
until you understand the lesson
it is trying to teach you.

April Green

make peace
with the space you are living within.

for this space is the bridge
that leads you to the person
you are becoming.

(this space is your life.)

honour your daily routine

if you don't yet have a goal, or a vision, then let it be your purpose to become the best version of yourself:

rise with the intention of self-care.

breathe fully. and strongly. and deeply.

replace an inherited belief with a new, positive belief.

get to know yourself again.

affirm that happiness, and love, and growth, all live in this very moment.

and remember:

where you are going, and who you are becoming is for you to decide.

April Green

the women i admire
the most
are the ones who fall,
and break, and hurt,
and ache;
yet still have the courage
to rise once more.

April Green

the wounds of the past
will not heal if you simply
forget about them.

they must be opened
and nurtured; so that they bloom.
and you grow from them.

April Green

you may have to kill many parts of your old self in order to survive.

never feel ashamed when a person questions your evolution:

"you've changed" is one of the most positive, life affirming statements you will ever hear.

April Green

how beautiful —
to look back at the storm
and the chaos and
watch yourself rising
from the wreckage.

when was the last time you honoured your own
strength?

April Green

you can be the sunlight
for other people too.

(growth isn't simply limited to yourself.)

April Green

self-love

self-love is like a feeling you have to carry around
with you for the rest of your life.

like your beating heart: it should never stop.

reaching the sun

the more you reach towards the person you are becoming, the less likely you are to fall back to the person you once were.

(stay committed to your journey of growth—don't allow the ego to keep you in your comfort zone.)

April Green

everything you are manifesting
(positive or negative),
is reminding you about all the things
you are thinking, feeling, and speaking about
the most.

.

April Green

something wild and beautiful happens
when you start to love yourself and
embrace every single piece of who you are.

i think it's something like freedom.

April Green

healing is
not just about forgiveness
or letting go.

healing is
the conscious, intentional exhale
full of new life
and
infinite potential
that creates a sacred space
for your evolving self to step into.

April Green

i can create who i want to be:
rediscover all the women inside me
allow love to bloom from the parts
i once denied
move my soul towards a sacred space
cleanse the past
honour my art
fall in love with moments
with people
with life

and still find the strength to dive into this soft body
and pull out the limiting beliefs holding me back.

April Green

that stillness
which breathes
and
has a pulse
and is alive
with life.

stay there for a moment longer.

no matter where i find myself:

may i always turn towards the things
that nourish my soul.

April Green

pain is a natural part of living.

but having the bravery to live with it,
learn from it, grow from it:

that is the most powerful gift
you can give yourself.

April Green

if the storm
does not pass:

breathe.

beautifully and tenderly.

for there is a language
on the breeze.
a language far deeper
than words.

and your soul will remember.

April Green

the soft revolution
that starts inside your heart
each time you feel your self-worth
diminishing.

April Green

if there is grace
in your heart
in your bones
in your breath:

you will always be beautiful.

April Green

waking dreams

when you tie your life to a dream, it's a breathtaking
and humbling experience to feel petals falling from
the sky into your hands like rain.

April Green

today

i will live in a sweetly, silent way
that says:

'i am here. this is the only voice i need.'

the lost life

please do not weep tears from the eyes of a lost life.
a life carved out for you on the breeze. a life walking
next to you, calling you, tugging at your soul; aching
for you to stand still and taste it.

take a leap of faith and step into this life.

and
there is still
time
to bloom.

(there will always be still time.)

April Green

unlearning

above all, become less of a human and more of a soul.

because life becomes easier when you stop being who they expect you to be.

WHEN INNER WISDOM

SPEAKS TO YOU:

LEAN INTO THAT SPACE AND

LISTEN.

— acknowledgements —

sasha, rachael, tina, xavier

&
a very special thank-you to my readers.

your love means more to me than you will ever
know.

love,
april green

instagram: @loveaprilgreen

www.bloomforyourself.co.uk